READ WELL®

Composition

Skill Book 2

Units 17–30

Cambium
LEARNING®

BOSTON, MA | LONGMONT, CO

3 4 5 6 7   RRDHRBVA   15 14 13 12 11

ISBN-13: 978-1-60697-146-8
ISBN-10: 1-60697-146-8

184410/5-11

Printed in the United States of America
Published and Distributed by

Cambium
LEARNING®
Sopris West®

4093 Specialty Place • Longmont, CO 80504 • 303-651-2829

www.voyagerlearning.com

ILLUSTRATION CREDITS:
21: Illustrated by Clark Tate.
33: Illustrated by Margo Burian

Table of Contents

Name _____

1 Most sharks eat meat.

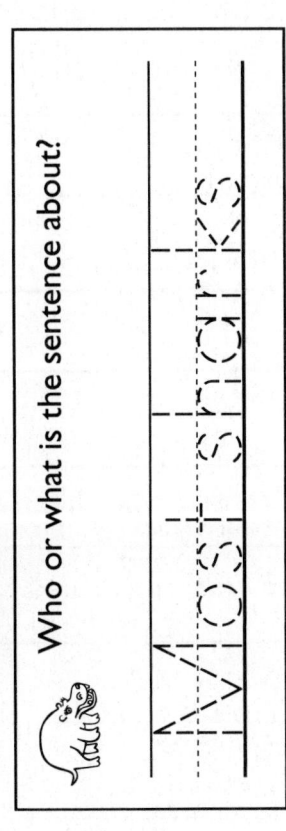

Who or what is the sentence about?

Most sharks

What does the sentence say about most sharks?
Most sharks . . .

eat meat

2 They are carnivores.

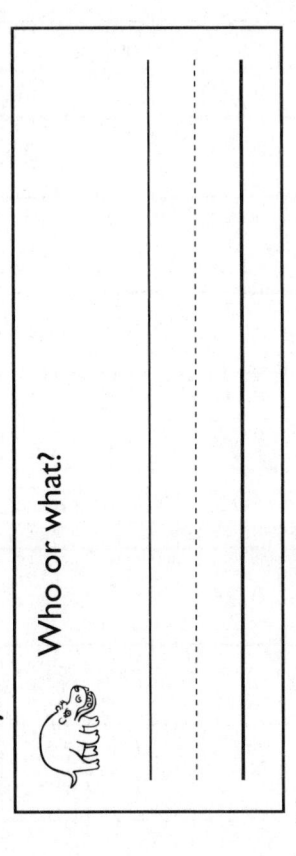

Who or what?

What does the sentence say about the sharks?
They . . .

3 They hunt for meat.

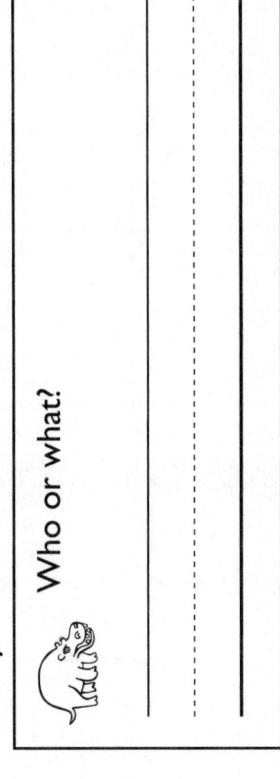

Who or what?

What does the sentence say about the sharks?
They . . .

Name _____

Have students trace and write each letter, following the arrows. Then have students trace and write "star."

1   our _____   star _____ _____ _____

Have students fill in the missing letters and then trace.

2   __ef   __hi   __k__   __no   __ar

Have students copy the letters from Row 2 and complete the happy face when they've done their best work.

3 _____

✔ and correct

Have students trace the shifty words and complete the happy face when they've done their best work.

4   arm   art   tart   start

✔ and correct

- - - - - ✂ -

Name _____

Have students trace each letter pattern. Then have students write the letters on their own.

1   ar   ar _____ _____ _____ _____

Have students trace the rhyming words and identify what's the same about them.

2   star   car   shark   Mark

Have students write the rhyming words from Row 2.

3 _____

Have students trace the sentence and identify the rhyming words.

4   See Mark the shark

Name _____

Have students trace the letter pattern and the words.

1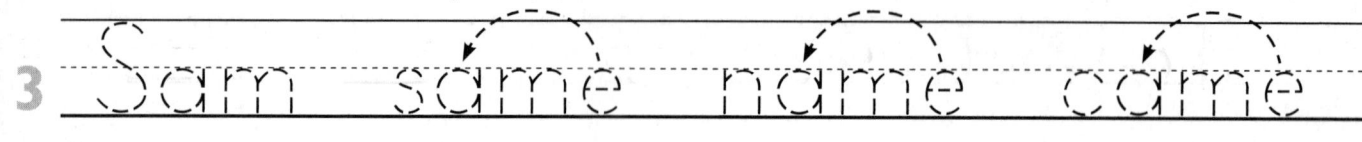

Have students write the letter pattern and words from Row 1.

2

Have students trace "Sam" and the Bossy E words and arrows.

3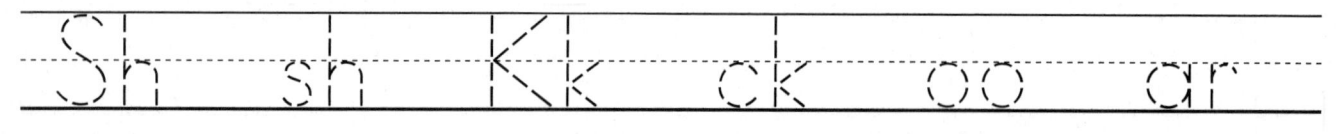

Have students write "Sam" and the Bossy E words from Row 3.

4

UNIT **17** SKILL WORK DAY 5
Handwriting

Name _____

Letter Review: Have students trace the letters.

1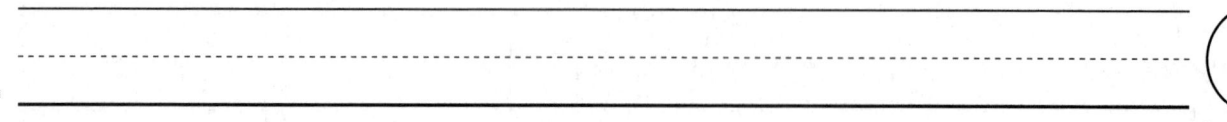

Have students write the letters from Row 1 and complete the happy face when they've done their best work.

2

✔ and correct

Have students trace and complete the sentence with a picture word.

3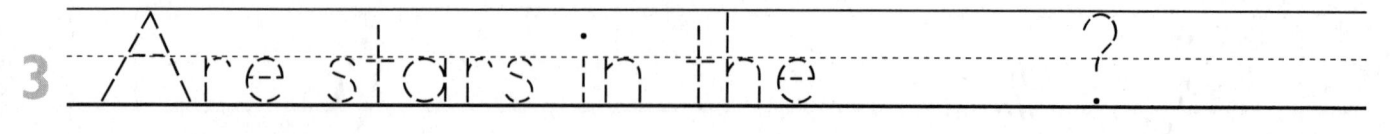

Have students write the sentence from Row 3.

4

Name _____

Have students draw a line through the misspelled Bossy E word and write the correct word above it. Then have students find a synonym for "very big" and write it in the blank. Finally, have students add a picture of a whale to the box and color the picture.

whale
The ~~what~~ is very big.

The whale is _____

The wale is _____

The whalle is _____

The wal is _____

Name _____

Have students trace and write the letter pattern, following the arrow. Then have students trace and write "wheat."

1 Wh _____ _____ wheat _____

Have students fill in the missing letters and then trace.

2 _hi _ki _no _gr _tu

Have students write the letters from Row 2 and complete the happy face when they've done their best work.

3 ghi jkl mno pqr stu   ☺ ✔ and correct

Have students trace the shifty words and complete the happy face when they've done their best work.

4 sank sand hand   ☺ ✔ and correct

- - - ✂ -

Name _____

Have students trace and write the letter pattern, following the arrow. Then have students trace and write "whoosh."

1 wh _____ _____ whoosh _____

Have students trace the rhyming words and identify what's the same about them.

2 hank stank thank

Have students write the rhyming words from Row 2 and complete the happy face when they've done their best work.

3 _____   ☺ ✔ and correct

Have students trace the phrase, identify the rhyming words, and complete the happy face when they've done their best work.

4 Hank in a tank   ☺ ✔ and correct

Have students trace each letter pattern and complete the happy face when they've done their best work.

1 Wh wh Wh wh

✔ and correct

Have students trace the words.

2 what are want

Have students write the words from Row 2 and complete the happy face when they've done their best work.

3

✔ and correct

Have students trace "mad" and the Bossy E words and arrows.

4 mad made make take

✂

Letter Review: Have students trace the letters.

1 Kk ck oo ar Wh wh

Have students write the letters from Row 1 and complete the happy face when they've done their best work.

2

✔ and correct

Have students trace and complete the sentences with a picture word.

3 What can I see? I can

4 see a _____ in the sea_

Name __Aaron__

Read the story to students.

●	■	▲
The little red dog was sad. He lost his bone.	He looked in the car. He looked in the sand.	He found it in his dish. Then the little red dog chewed all day long.

Guide students as they fill out the story map.

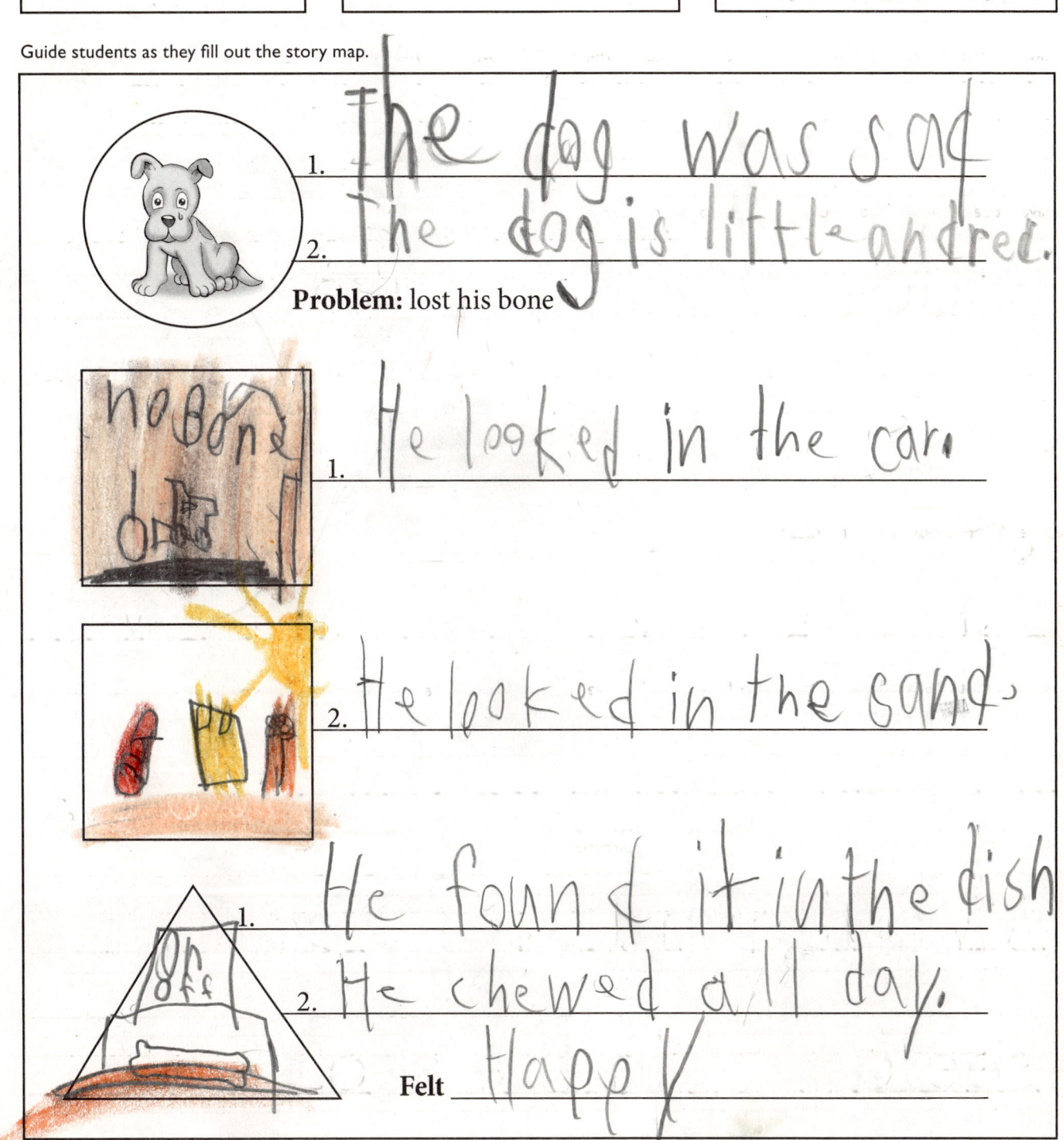

1. The dog was sad

2. The dog is little and red.

Problem: lost his bone

1. He looked in the car.

2. He looked in the sand.

1. He found it in the dish

2. He chewed all day.

Felt Happy

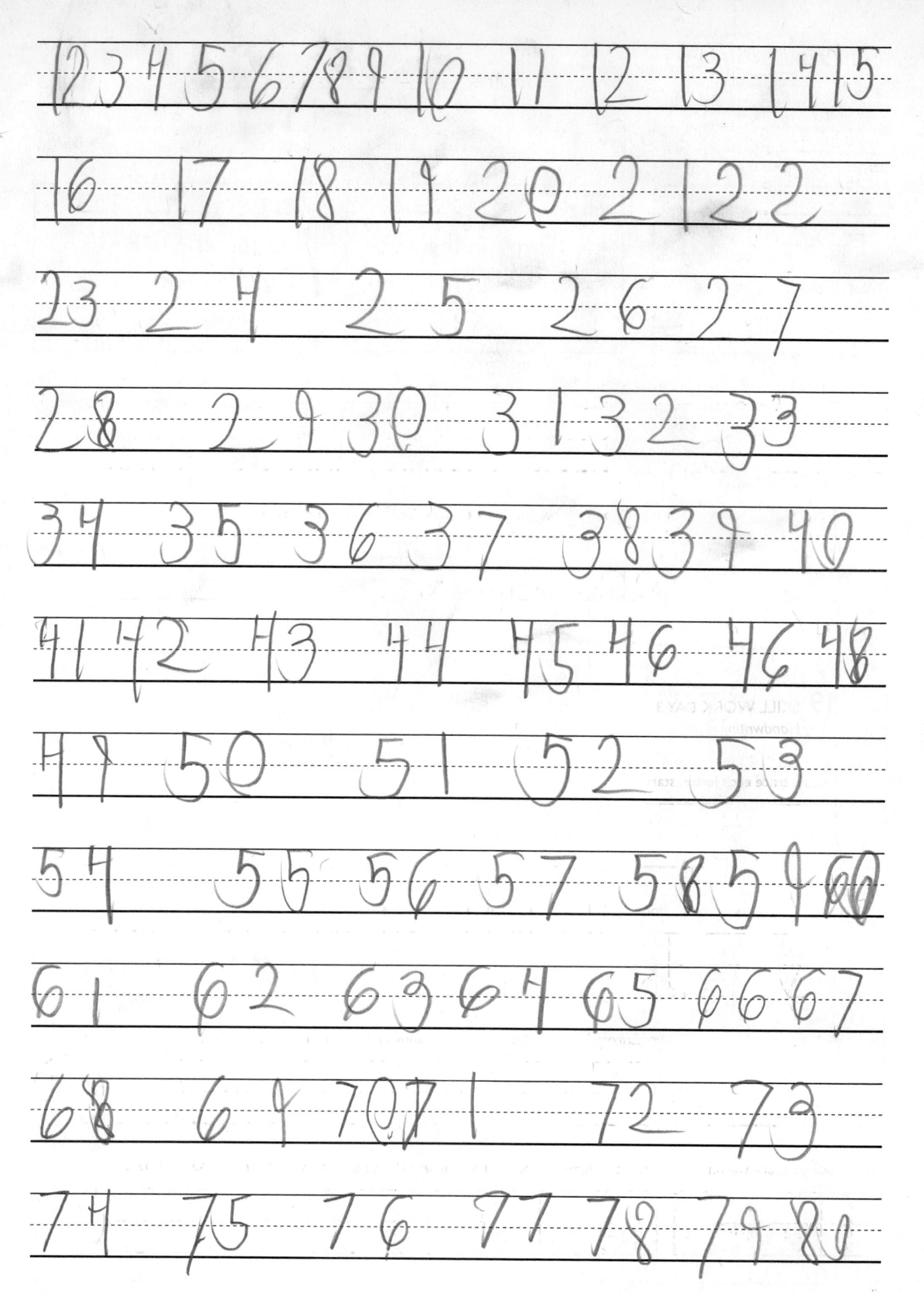

1 2 3 4 5 6 7 8 9 10 11 12 13 14 15

16 17 18 19 20 21 22

23 24 25 26 27

28 29 30 31 32 33

34 35 36 37 38 39 40

41 42 43 44 45 46 47 48

49 50 51 52 53

54 55 56 57 58 59 60

61 62 63 64 65 66 67

68 69 70 71 72 73

74 75 76 77 78 79 80

10

Name _____

Have students trace each letter, starting at the dot and following the arrow. Then have students write the letters on their own.

1 E E ___ ___ ___ e e ___ ___ ___

Have students fill in the missing letters and then trace.

2 _k l ___n o ___g r ___t u ___w x

Have students write the letters from Row 2.

3

Have students trace the shifty words and complete the happy face when they've done their best work.

4 hen   ten   then   when

✔ and correct

✂ -

Name _____

Have students trace each letter, starting at the dot and following the arrow. Then have students write the letters on their own.

1 w w ___ ___ ___ ___

Have students trace the rhyming words and identify what's the same about them.

2 sky   dry   try   shed   red

Have students write the rhyming words from Row 2 and complete the happy face when they've done their best work.

3

✔ and correct

Have students trace the phrase, identify the rhyming words, and complete the happy face when they've done their best work.

4 fly in the sky

✔ and correct

Have students trace the words.

1
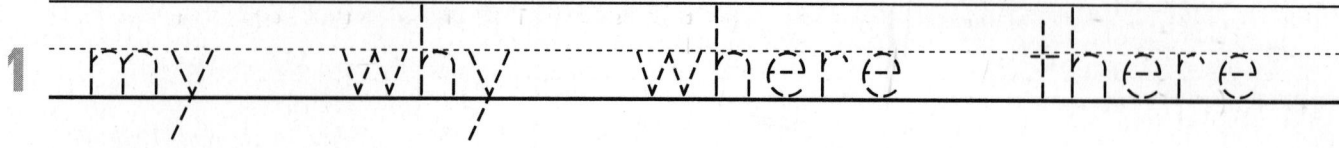

Have students write the words from Row 2.

2

Have students trace the Bossy <u>E</u> words and arrows.

3
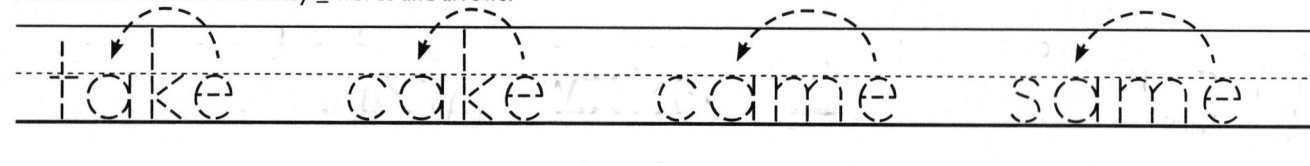

Have students write the Bossy <u>E</u> words from Row 3.

4

Letter Review: Have students trace the letters.

1
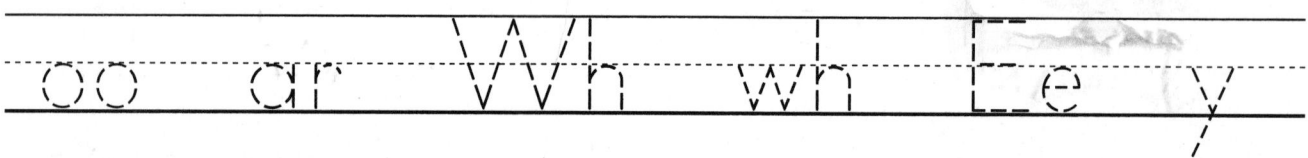

Have students write the letters from Row 1 and complete the happy face when they've done their best work.

2
✔ and correct

Have students trace and complete the sentences with a picture word and complete the happy face when they've done their best work.

3
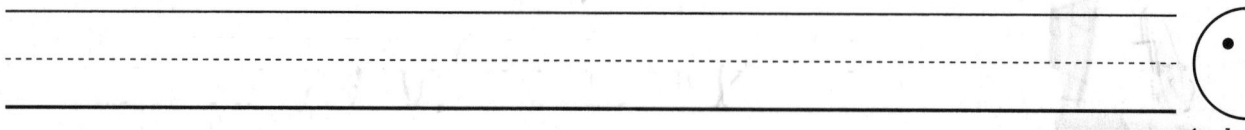

4
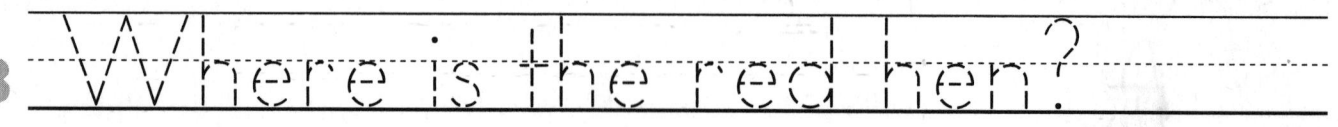
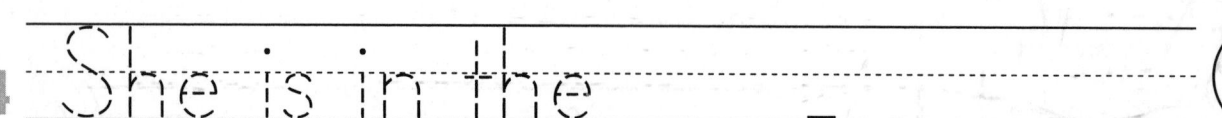

✔ and correct

Name  Aaron

Read the letter to students. Then guide students as they complete the second letter.

1-10-2009

Dear Grandma,
    Thank you for the book.
It is awesome. I like to
read about insects.
    School is fun. I am
learning how to write
letters.

    Love,
    Zeke

Date 12/29/14

Dear Grandma,
    Thank you for the
book. It is awesome.
I like to read about
insects.
    I school is fun.
I am learning to writ
letters. Love,
Zeke

Name _____

Read the story to students. Then guide students through the checklist. Have students complete the final copy.

Good Job Checklist

Good Job! ★ ★ ★

Organization

1. ____ The beginning tells what happened first.
2. ____ The middle tells what happened next.
3. ____ The end tells what happened last.
4. ____ The last sentence puts a finish on the story.

Ideas and Content

1. ____ The story tells about a fun day.
2. ____ Each part has at least two sentences.

Dan and Me
by Zelda

It was a fun day for Dan and me. First, we met at the park. When it was time to go home, we rode our bikes. It was a great day for Dan and me.
At the park, we played catch. We hit the ball. We ran fast.

Dan and Me

It was a fun day for Dan and me. First, we met at the park.

At the park, we played

catch. We hit the ball. We

ran fast.

Name _____

Have students trace each letter, starting at the dot and following the arrow. Then have students write the letter on their own.

1   O O O ___ ___ ___ ___ ___

Have students fill in the missing letters and then trace.

2 __ B C __ __ E F __ __ H I __ __ K L

Have students write the letters from Row 2 and complete the happy face when they've done their best work.

3 _____ ☺

✔ and correct

Have students trace the shifty words.

4 shoot sheet shot not

- - - - - - - - - - - - - - - - - - - ✂ -

Name _____

Have students trace each letter, starting at the dot and following the arrow. Then have students write the letter on their own.

1   o o o ___ ___ ___ ___ ___

Have students trace the rhyming words and identify what's the same about them.

2 rock sock lock

Have students write the rhyming words from Row 2 and complete the happy face when they've done their best work.

3 _____ ☺

✔ and correct

Have students trace the phrases and rhyming words.

4 not a lot that hot spot

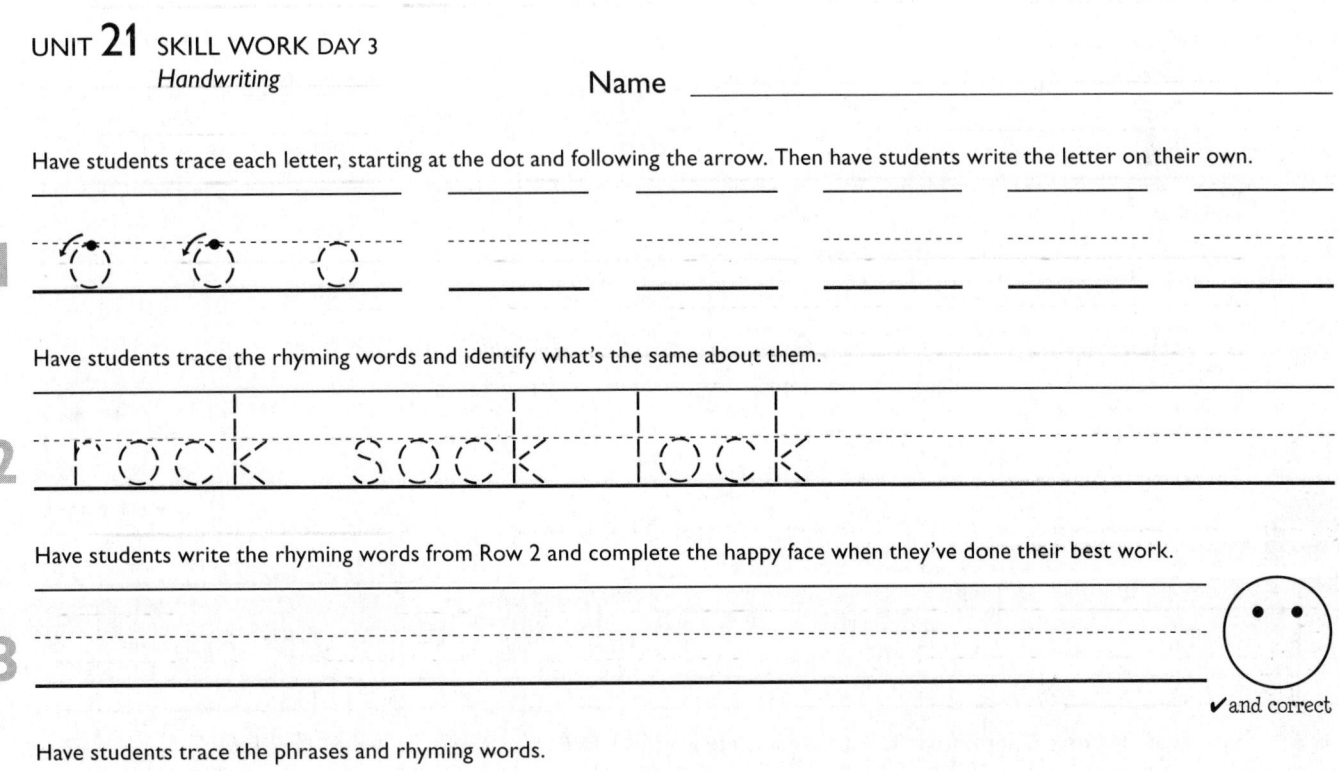

Name _____

Have students trace each letter set and complete the happy face when they've done their best work.

1 Oo Oo Oo Oo

✔ and correct

Have students trace the words.

2 what who where they

Have students write the words from Row 2 and complete the happy face when they've done their best work.

3

✔ and correct

Have students complete the sentence with a picture word, then complete the happy face when they've done their best work.

4 Who is in the

✔ and correct

✂

Name _____

Letter Review: Have students trace the letters.

1 Wh wh Ee y Ll Oo

Have students write the letters from Row 1 and complete the happy face when they've done their best work.

2

✔ and correct

Have students trace the Bossy E words and arrows.

3 like line time side

Have students write the Bossy E words from Row 3 and complete the happy face when they've done their best work.

4

✔ and correct

Focus Lesson:
Word Choice and Onomatopoeia

Name _____

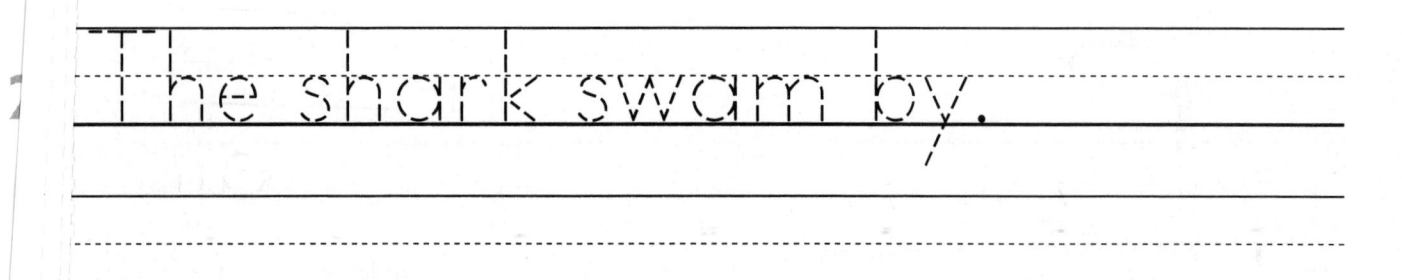

bzzz   hisss   thud   beep

thump   swoosh   plop

e students trace the sentence, then trace or write a second sentence composed of words that make sounds.

1   See the bee. Bzzz, bzzz, bzzz.

2   The shark swam by.

    The dog jumped off the bed.

Have students trace each letter, starting at the dot and following the arrow. Then have students write the letter on their own.

1 F F F _____ _____ _____ _____ _____

Have students fill in the missing letters and then trace.

2 __ K L __ __ N O __ Q R __ T U

Have students write the letters from Row 2.

3 _____

Have students trace the shifty words and complete the happy face when they've done their best work.

4 lost last fast fact

✔ and correct

- -

Have students trace each letter, starting at the dot and following the arrow. Then have students write the letter on their own.

1 f f f _____ _____ _____ _____ _____

Have students trace the rhyming words and identify what's the same about the words.

2 sang rang fine mine

Have students trace the sentence and identify the rhyming words, then complete the happy face when they've done their best work.

3 The big fish on that line

4 is mine

✔ and correct

Name _____

Have students trace each letter set and complete the happy face when they've done their best work.

1 Ff Ff Ff Ff

✔ and correct

Have students trace the words.

2 work because one two

Have students write the words from Row 2.

3

Have students trace the Bossy **E** words and arrows, then complete the happy face when they've done their best work.

4 hose nose rose note

✔ and correct

- ✂ - - - -

UNIT **24** SKILL WORK DAY 5
Handwriting

Name _____

Letter Review: Have students trace the letters.

1 Oo Bb all Gg Ff

Have students write the letters from Row 1 and complete the happy face when they've done their best work.

2

✔ and correct

Have students trace and complete the sentence with a picture word and complete the happy face when they've done their best work.

3 Did that frog fly into

4 the _____

✔ and correct

32

Have students trace the words first, next, then, and finally on the cycle graph, then trace and complete the sentences below the graph that describe the life cycle of a butterfly.

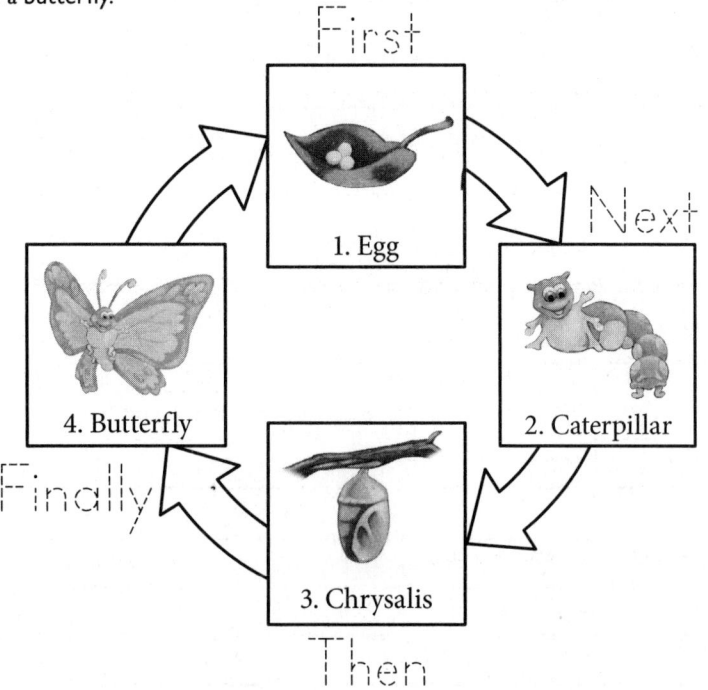

1 First, there is an egg.

2 _____ a caterpillar

hatches.

3 _____ a chrysalis forms.

4 _____ a butterfly

emerges.

Copyright 2010 Cambium Learning Sopris West®. All rights reserved.

UNIT **25** SKILL WORK DAY 2
Handwriting

Name _____

Have students trace each letter, starting at the dot and following the arrow. Then have students write the letter on their own.

1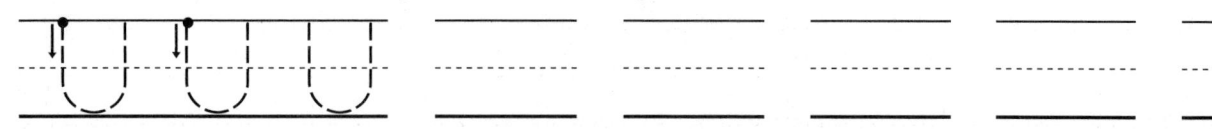

Have students fill in the missing letters and then trace.

2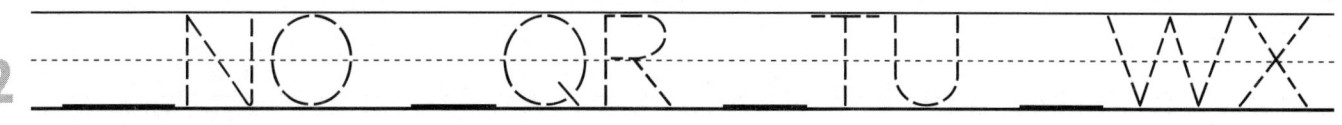

Have students write the letters from Row 2.

3

Have students trace the shifty words and complete the happy face when they've done their best work.

4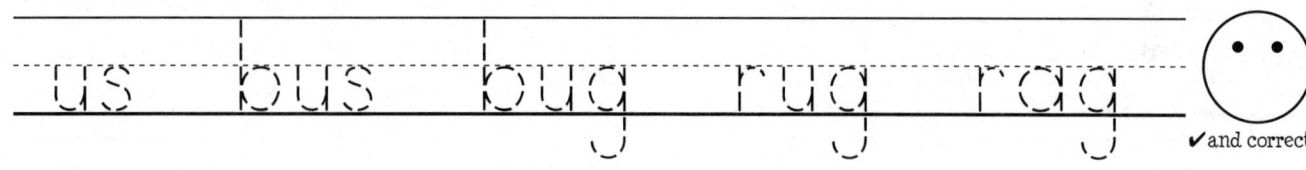

✔ and correct

✂ -

UNIT **25** SKILL WORK DAY 3
Handwriting

Name _____

Have students trace each letter, starting at the dot and following the arrow. Then have students write the letter on their own.

1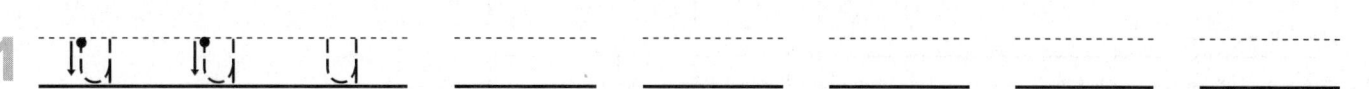

Have students trace the rhyming words and identify what's the same about the words.

2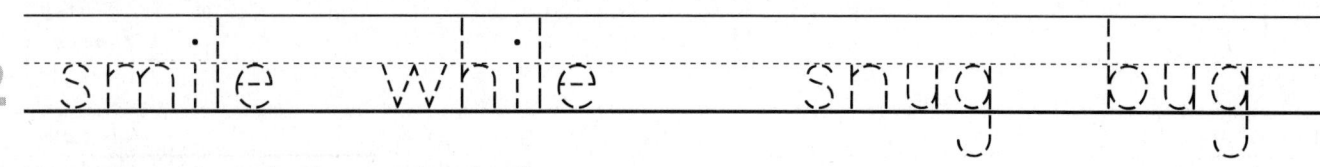

Have students write the rhyming words from Row 2.

3

Have students trace the phrase and identify the rhyming words.

4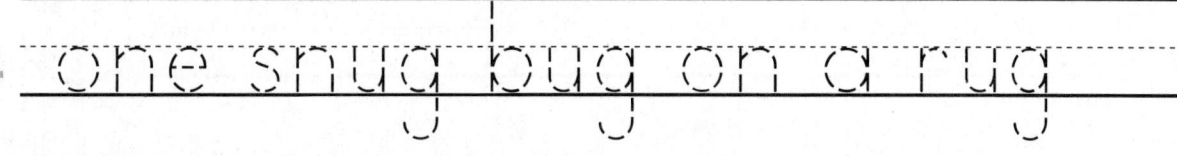

Have students trace each letter set and complete the happy face when they've done their best work.

1   Uu   Uu   Uu   Uu

✔and correct

Have students trace the words.

2   from   worked   working

Have students write the words from Row 2.

3

Have students trace the Bossy E words and arrows.

4   hole   stone   nose   rose

UNIT **25** SKILL WORK DAY 5
Handwriting

Name _____

Letter Review: Have students trace the letters.

1   Bb all Gg Ff Uu

Have students write the letters from Row 1 and complete the happy face when they've done their best work.

2

✔and correct

Have students trace and complete the sentence with a picture word and complete the happy face when they've done their best work.

3   I am working hard on

4   my ___

✔and correct

Name _____

For each passage, read the story, then guide students through the checklist.

Draft 1

Bill

This is Bill. He is seven. Bill plays ball. Bill hits the ball. Then, he runs the bases. Bill is a star.

Good Job Checklist

Good Job! ★ ★ ★

Organization

1. ___ The beginning introduces the main character.
2. ___ The middle tells what happens.
3. ___ The end wraps up the story.

Ideas and Content

1. ___ The story tells all about the main character.
2. ___ Each part has at least two sentences.

Great Job! ★ ★ ★ ★

Word Choice

1. ___ The story has a snazzy word or two.
2. ___ The story has rhyming words, repetition, words that make sounds, or a simile.

Draft 2

Bill

This is Bill. He is seven. Bill plays ball. Bill hits the ball. He whacks it hard. Then, he runs the bases. Zoom, zoom, zoom! Bill is incredible. He is a star.

Good Job Checklist

Good Job! ★ ★ ★

Organization

1. ___ The beginning introduces the main character.
2. ___ The middle tells what happens.
3. ___ The end wraps up the story.

Ideas and Content

1. ___ The story tells all about the main character.
2. ___ Each part has at least two sentences.

Great Job! ★ ★ ★ ★

Word Choice

1. ___ The story has a snazzy word or two.
2. ___ The story has rhyming words, repetition, words that make sounds, or a simile.

For Passage 2, have students find and underline the words that make sounds—"whacks" and "zoom, zoom, zoom." Then have students find and circle the snazzy word "incredible." Have students write the words on the lines below.

Snazzy Words and Words that Make a Sound:

_____

_____

_____

_____

Have students trace, then write the u-r letter pattern. Then have students trace and write "her."

1 er ___ ___ her ___ ___ ___

Have students fill in the missing letters and then trace.

2 __QR __TU __WX __Z

Have students write the letters from Row 2.

3

Have students trace the shifty words and complete the happy face when they've done their best work.

4 mister sister sitter

✔ and correct

Have students trace, then write the o-o letter pattern. Then have students trace and write "book."

1 oo ___ ___ book ___ ___

Have students trace the rhyming words and identify what's the same about the words.

2 look cook song long

Have students write the rhyming words from Row 2.

3

Have students trace the sentence and identify the rhyming words.

4 She sang a long song

Name _____

Have students trace each letter pattern and complete the happy face when they've done their best work.

1 er   er   er   oo   oo   oo   ✔ and correct

Have students trace the words.

2 other   brother   mother

Have students write the words from Row 2.

3

Have students trace the Bossy <u>E</u> words and arrows, then complete the happy face when they've done their best work.

4 game   mine   bone   ✔ and correct

Name _____

Letter Review: Have students trace the letters.

1 Gg   Ff   Uu   er   oo

Have students write the letters from Row 1 and complete the happy face when they've done their best work.

2   ✔ and correct

Have students trace and complete the sentence with a picture word.

3 Yesterday, my sister and

4 I were on the ___

Focus Lesson:
Commas in a Series

Name _____

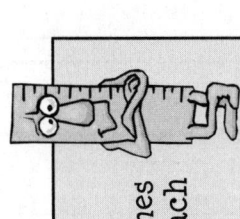

Commas in a List Rule:
If you have three or more names in a list, put a comma after each name (except the last!).

Underline the names. Then add commas as appropriate.

1. My friends are Sam and Tim.

2. My friends are Sam Tim and Ann.

3. My friends are Sam Tim Ann and Jan.

Read and write each sentence. Complete the last sentence with the people who make up your family.

1 In my family are <u>Mom and I.</u>

_____

_____

2 In my family are my <u>dad</u>, my <u>sister</u>, and <u>I.</u>

_____

_____

3 In my family are . . .

_____

_____

Have students trace each letter, starting at the dot and following the arrow. Then have students write the letters on their own.

1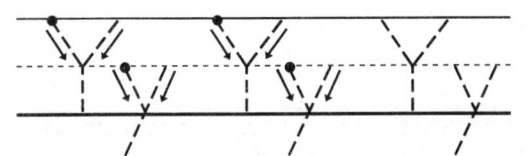

Have students fill in the missing letters and then trace.

2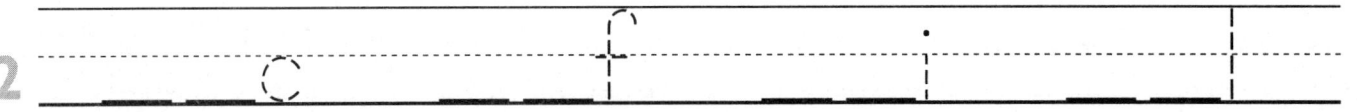

Have students write the letters from Row 2 and complete the happy face when they've done their best work.

3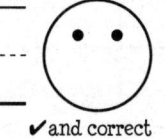

✔ and correct

Have students trace the shifty words and complete the happy face when they've done their best work.

4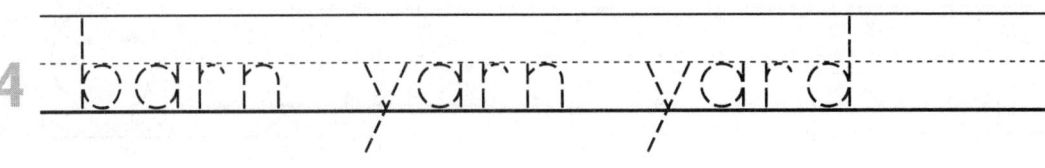

✔ and correct

Have students trace each letter, starting at the dot and following the arrow. Then have students write the letters on their own.

1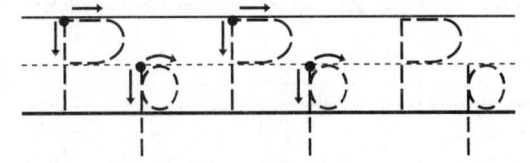

Have students trace the rhyming words and identify what's the same about the words.

2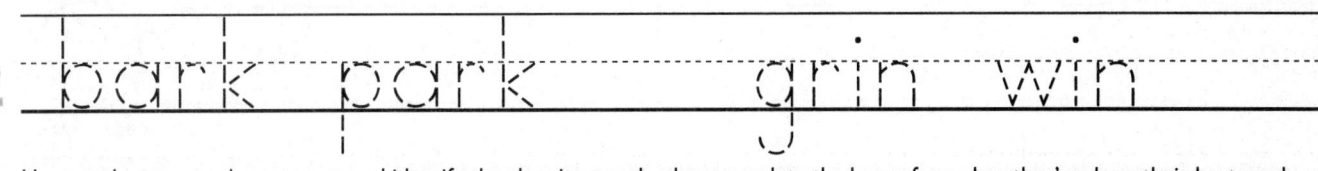

Have students trace the sentence and identify the rhyming words, then complete the happy face when they've done their best work.

3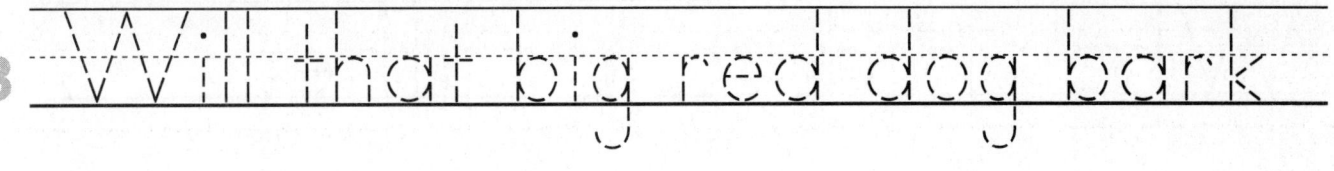

4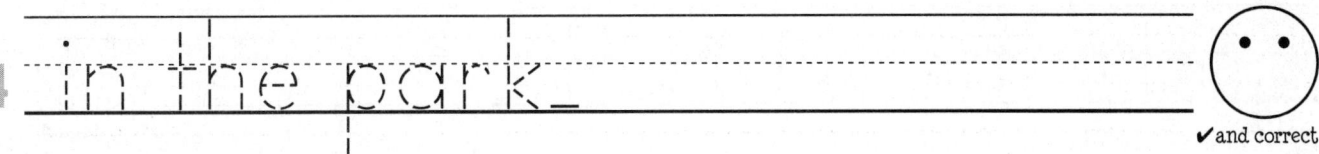

✔ and correct

Name _____

Have students trace each letter set and complete the happy face when they've done their best work.

1 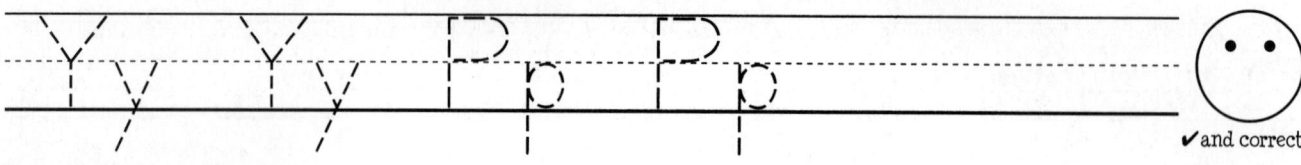   ✔ and correct

Have students trace the words.

2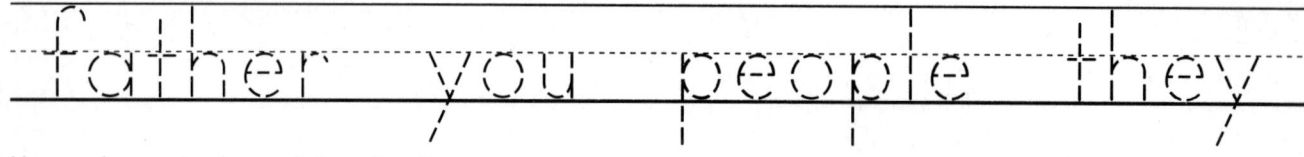

Have students write the words from Row 2.

3

Have students trace the Bossy <u>E</u> words and arrows.

4 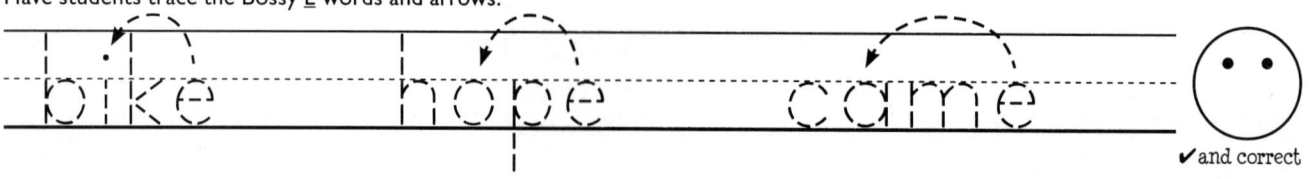   ✔ and correct

---

UNIT **27** SKILL WORK DAY 5
Handwriting

Name _____

Letter Review: Have students trace the letters.

1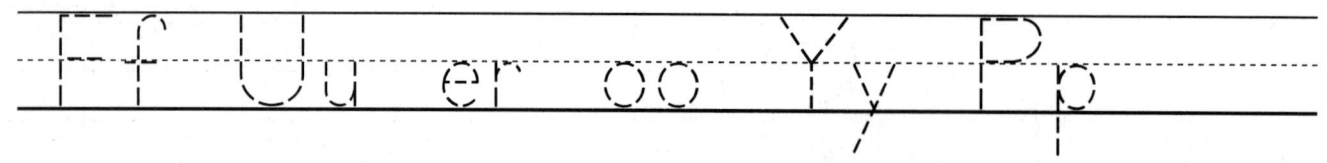

Have students write the letters from Row 1 and complete the happy face when they've done their best work.

2   ✔ and correct

Have students trace the sentence and complete the happy face when they've done their best work.

3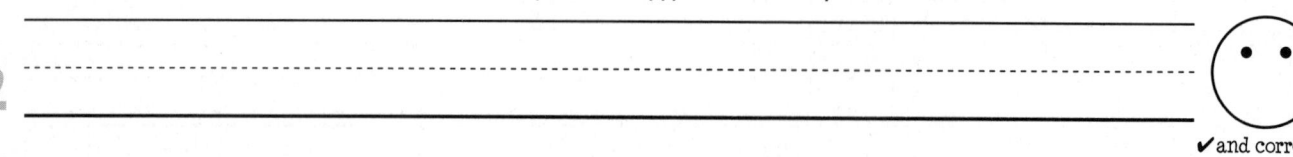

4 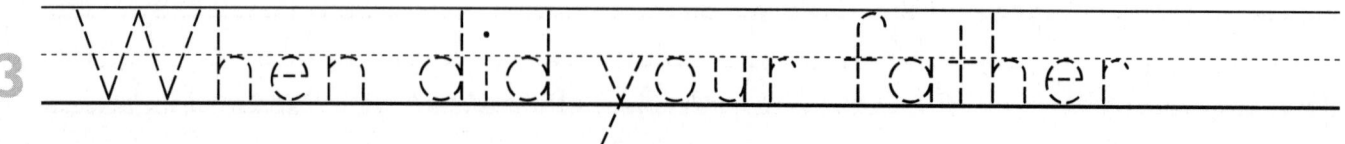   ✔ and correct

Focus Lesson:
Word Choice and
Snazzy Action Words

Name _____

Read the sentences in each box with students. Have students identify which sentence is more interesting and circle the snazzy action word.

Box 1	Box 2
A snake <u>went</u> by.  A snake <u>slithered</u> by.	The cat <u>jumped</u>.  The cat <u>pounced</u>.

Have students trace the sentences, then circle the snazzy action words.

1 The monkey <u>goes</u> from tree to tree.

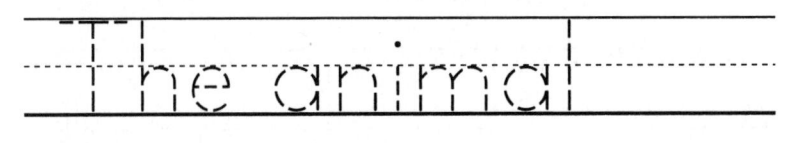

The monkey swings
from tree to tree.

2 The animal <u>eats</u> grass.

The animal

munches on grass.

3 The bat <u>flies</u> over the river.

The bat swoops over

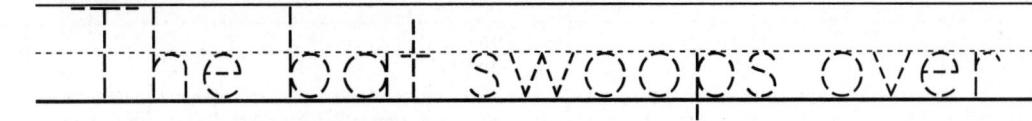

the river.

UNIT 28 SKILL WORK DAY 2
Handwriting

Name _____

Have students trace each letter, starting at the dot and following the arrow. Then have students write the letters on their own.

1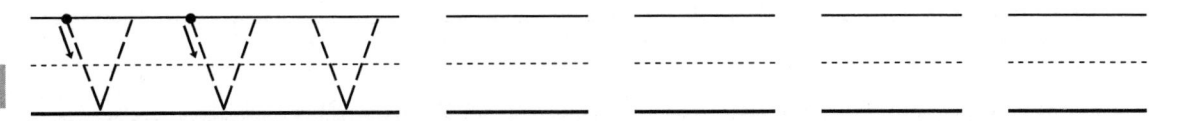

Have students fill in the missing letters and then trace.

2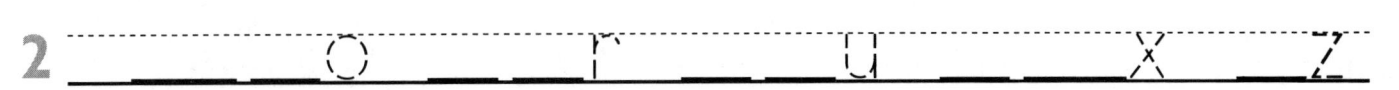

Have students write the letters from Row 2 and complete the happy face when they've done their best work.

3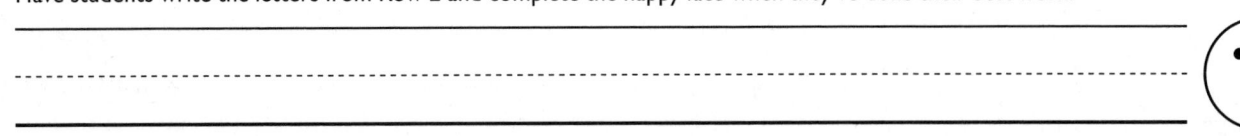

✔ and correct

Have students trace the shifty words and complete the happy face when they've done their best work.

4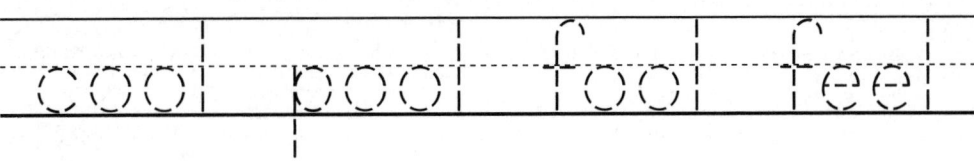

✔ and correct

UNIT 28 SKILL WORK DAY 3
Handwriting

Name _____

Have students trace each letter, starting at the dot and following the arrow. Then have students write the letters on their own.

1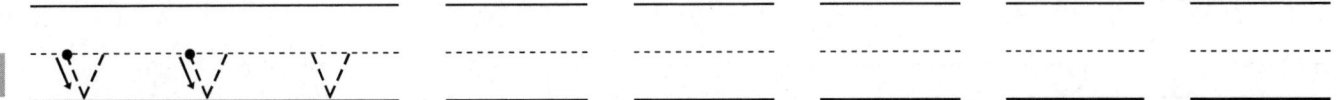

Have students trace the rhyming words and identify what's the same about the words.

2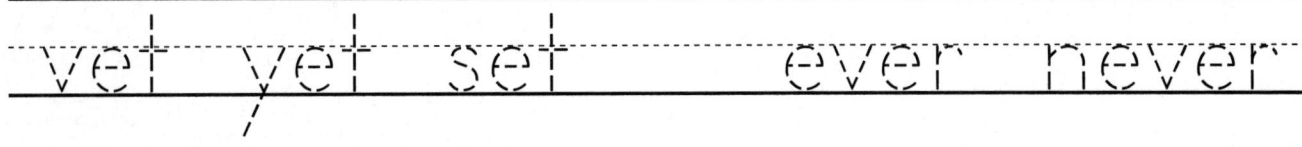

Have students write the rhyming words from Row 2.

3

Have students trace the sentence and identify the rhyming words.

4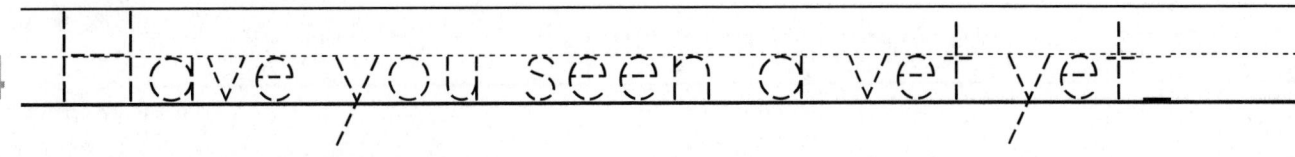

Name _____

Have students trace each letter set and complete the happy face when they've done their best work.

1 Vv Vv Vv Vv Vv

✔ and correct

Have students trace the words.

2 live give of have

Have students write the words from Row 2.

3

Have students trace the Bossy <u>E</u> words and arrows, then complete the happy face when they've done their best work.

4 hope plate fire

✔ and correct

✂ --

Name _____

Letter Review: Have students trace the letters.

1 Uu er oo Yy Pp Vv

Have students write the letters from Row 1 and complete the happy face when they've done their best work.

2

✔ and correct

Have students trace and complete the sentence with a picture word and complete the happy face when they've done their best work.

3 There are two hundred

4 in the river_

✔ and correct

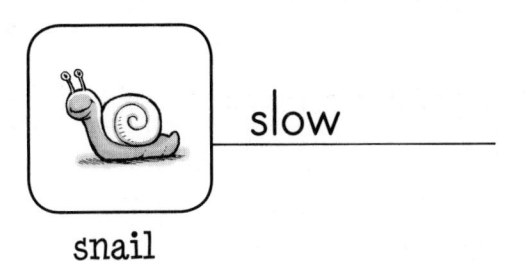

snail — slow

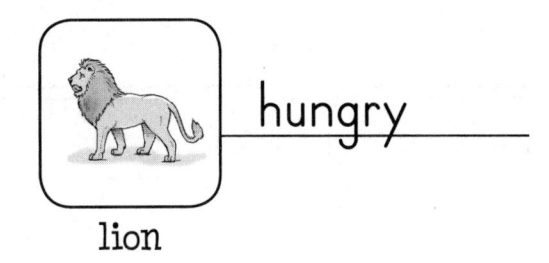

lion — hungry

old dog — slow

Simile 1

The old dog was as slow

snake — hungry

Simile 2

The green snake was as

hungry

Have students trace each letter, starting at the dot and following the arrow. Then have the students write the letters on their own.

1 Qu Qu Qu ____ ____ ____

Have students fill in the missing letters and then trace.

2 ____ C ____ F ____ I ____ L

Have students write the letters from Row 2.

3

Have students trace the shifty words and complete the happy face when they've done their best work.

4 quack quick quit

✔and correct

- -

UNIT **29** SKILL WORK DAY 3
Handwriting

Name _____

Have students trace each letter, starting at the dot and following the arrow. Then have the students write the letters on their own.

1 qu qu qu ____ ____ ____

Have students trace the rhyming words and identify what's the same about the words.

2 quake shake bake

Have students write the rhyming words from Row 2.

3

Have students trace the phrase and identify the rhyming words.

4 quake and shake

Have students trace each letter pattern and complete the happy face when they've done their best work.

1 Qu qu Qu qu   ☺ ✔ and correct

Have students trace the words.

2 come some boys please

Have students write the words from Row 2.

3

Have students trace the Bossy **E** words and arrows, then complete the happy face when they've done their best work.

4 quake five rope   ☺ ✔ and correct

- ✂

Letter Review: Have students trace the letters.

1 er oo Yy Pp Vv Qu qu

Have students write the letters from Row 1.

2

Have students trace the sentence.

3 The boys quit working

4 and dove into the pool.

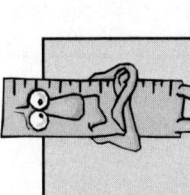

Commas in a List Rule:
If you have three or more things in a list, put a comma after each (except the last!).

Name _____

Underline the animal names. Then add commas as appropriate.

1. Tamarind monkeys and harpy eagles are endangered.

2. Tamarind monkeys harpy eagles and some toucans are endangered.

3. Tamarind monkeys harpy eagles some toucans and poison dart frogs are endangered.

Read and write each sentence. Complete the last sentence with a list of your favorite rain forest animals.

1 <u>Jaguars</u> and <u>tapirs</u> live in the rain forest.

_____

- -

_____

2 <u>Jaguars</u>, <u>tapirs</u>, and <u>sloths</u> live in the rain forest.

_____

- -

_____

3 My three favorite rain forest animals are . . .

_____

- -

_____

Copyright 2010 Cambium Learning Sopris West®. All rights reserved.

Name _____

Have students trace each letter, starting at the dot and following the arrow. Then have the students write the letters on their own.

1 J J J _____ _____ _____

Have students fill in the missing letters and then trace.

2 O R U X

Have students write the letters from Row 2.

3 _____

Have students trace the shifty words and complete the happy face when they've done their best work.

4 damp dump jump ☺

✔ and correct

Name _____

Have students trace each letter, starting at the dot and following the arrow. Then have students write the letters on their own.

1 j j j _____ _____ _____

Have students trace the letter pattern and rhyming words and identify what's the same about the words.

2 ay say way play

Have students write the letter pattern and rhyming words from Row 2 and complete the happy face when they've done their best work.

3 _____ ☺

✔ and correct

Have students trace the sentence and identify the rhyming words.

4 May I play today_

Have students trace each letter set and complete the happy face when they've done their best work.

1 Jj Jj Jj Jj Jj

✔ and correct

Have students trace the words.

2 very   friend   from   your

Have students write the words from Row 2.

3

Have students trace the Bossy <u>E</u> words and arrows, then complete the happy face they've done their best work.

4 quite   quote   name

✔ and correct

- ✂ - -

Letter Review: Have students trace the letters.

1 Yy Pp Vv Qu qu Jj jay

Have students write the letters from Row 1.

2

Have students trace and complete the sentence with a picture word.

3 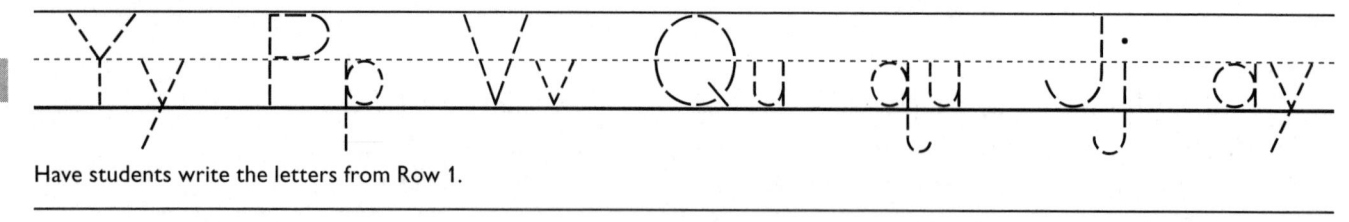 Jack drove his jeep deep

4 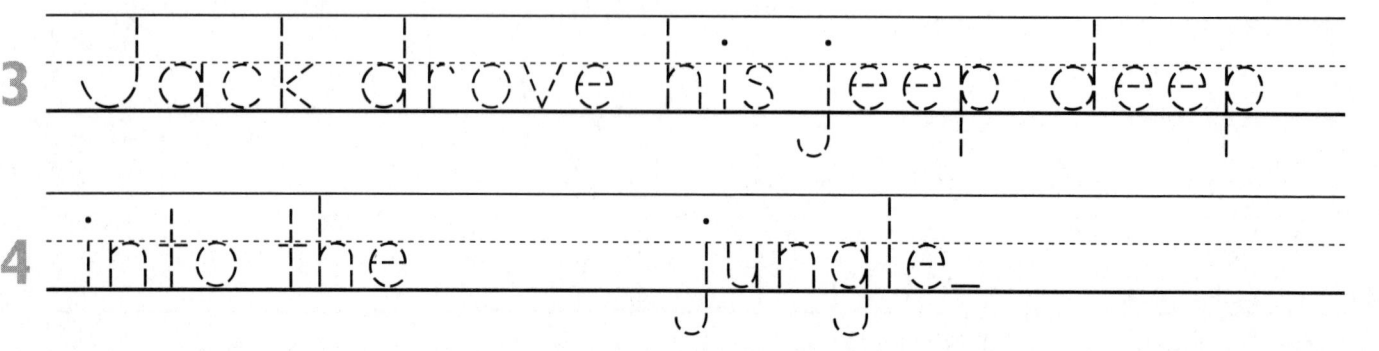 into the   jungle_